Potscrubber Lullabies

D1132727

Potscrubber Lullabies

Eric McHenry

For Niki and Ido,
In red, the better
to emphasize my
gratitude for your
friendship,

[signature]

WAYWISER

First published in 2006 by

THE WAYWISER PRESS

9 Woodstock Road, London N4 3ET, UK
P.O. Box 6205, Baltimore, MD 21206, USA
www.waywiser-press.com

Managing Editor
Philip Hoy

Associate Editors
Joseph Harrison   Clive Watkins   Greg Williamson

A CIP catalogue record for this book is available from the British Library

ISBN-10: 1-904130-22-4
ISBN-13: 978-1-904130-22-2

Printed and bound by
Cromwell Press Ltd., Trowbridge, Wiltshire

For Sonja, Evan and Mimi

Acknowledgements

Thanks to the editors of the following magazines for publishing my poems, some of which first appeared in slightly different form:

American Literary Review: "Vanguard"; *Bat City Review*: "Hyper-Mart"; *Cranky*: "Point Lobos," "Potscrubber Lullabies"; *Dogwood*: "Sitting on Jane Kenyon's Headstone"; *Harvard Review*: '"No Matter What",' '"Please Please Me",' "The Sign"; *Literary Imagination*: "West Concord," "Let Me Get This Straight"; *LitRag*: "The Rows," '"She's Gone",' "Notes Toward a Letter to Ed," "Misreading Pennsylvania," "Fire Diary," "Bird Plays to a Cow," "What I Think"; *The New Republic*: "Rebuilding Year," "The Novel"; *No: a journal of the arts*: "On the Smokestack"; *Northwest Review*: '"Brick House",' "*McHenry Replies:*," "Me and My Epoch," "My Solipsism Is Superior to Yours"; *Orion:* "No Daughter"; *Poet Lore*: "How to Write Autobiography"; *Slate*: "Borrowing Milky-White for the St Paul's Student Production of *Into the Woods*," "Figurative North Topeka."

Contents

Rebuilding Year

My Solipsism Is Superior to Yours

Contents

The Outstruments Are In

"The similarities among human music, bird song, and whale song tempt one to speculate that the Platonic alternative may exist – that there is a universal music awaiting discovery."

– Patricia Gray et al., *Science* magazine

"Why is it, I said to myself one night, that listening to the music I feel a homesickness for a vanished world that I was never a part of?"

– Charles Simic

Rebuilding Year

Rebuilding Year

After Beloit I went back to the paper
and wrote arts features for eight dollars an hour,
and lived in the Gem Building, on the block between
Topeka High with its Gothic tower
and the disheveled Statehouse with its green
dome of oxidizing copper.

I was sorry that I had no view
of old First National. Something obscured it
from my inset balcony. I heard it
imploding, though, like Kansas Avenue
clearing its throat, and saw the gaudy brown
dust-edifice that went up when it came down.

Friday nights I walked to High's home games
and sat high in the bleachers,
and tried to look like a self-knowing new
student, and tried not to see my teachers,
and picked out players with familiar names
and told them what to do.

The Incumbent

A root with no apparent
source is shouldering
up through the incoherent,
ash-rich soil in which
J.C. Hebbard's body
lies a-mouldering,

and may topple his
eye-high obelisk.
Its attitude already
registers the breach.

He made one modest run
for secretary of state,
pulling about fifteen
percent, like every Green-
back Labor candidate,

signed on as Sockless Jerry
Simpson's secretary
and rode the Populist
groundswell to Washington,

then came home to this last
unelected office.
That's one thing cemeteries
have going for them: low
turnover, and yet here he's
about to be unseated
by the one errant surface
root of a distant oak.

Down there among the others,
his casket-husk must look

like a dismasted ship
or sperm whale in the grip
of something legendary.

My great-great-great-grandfather's
monument takes a bow,
and threatens, with the shadow
of its attenuated
capital, the rest
of his west-tending row.

I love this cemetery's
asymmetries, although
it must be hell to mow.

The Sign

The memory of the just is blessed
but by whom and of the just what?
Infinite words are in the stone.
These were the seven someone cut
out of it. Now a damper, darker
element is almost done
replacing them with lichen crust.

A burly oak whose root-tips must
be fingering his collarbone
rains acorns on my rental car.
What if J.C. Hebbard's marker,
rather than the tree, had grown?

Then another stone, not far
from his, inscribed *God's Little Power
Ranger* (it exists), would tower
protectively over their half-acre,

and the McDonald's sign would pull
free of its anchor bolts and rise,
beating its arches, and patrol
southwest Topeka from the skies,
and do superheroic things
for justice's sake, instead of just
announcing WE HAVE MIGHTY WINGS.

HyperMart

It's the largest Wal-Mart in the plains states.
Some of the stockers are on rollerskates.
Adam wears a laminated tag,
ADAM, and a badge, HELLO.
He puts my bag of pretzels in a bag.

Back in Elmhurst, an airplane bungalow
is aging like a person – accomplishing years
in months, imposing itself upon its beams,
breathing out and opening its seams.
Gutters congest. Grey paint comes off in spears
revealing bits of old identities.
A strip of eccentric yellow reappears.

Thirty years ago, Dutch Elm Disease
stumped Elmhurst. But on a nylon banner
some preservationist or civic planner
drew up, the elm is unmistakable.
It bellies from the gable
of every sixth or seventh porch.
The canopy makes a sheltering arch
over the legend,

> Good Neighbors Through Time
> Since 1909.

I like it: one companionable line
and then another – iamb, anapest / iamb,
anapest, and that unassuming rhyme –
but what I want is a shirt:
You take the elms from Elmhurst, you get hurt.

Provincial

Is or isn't Burma Myanmar?
Here at the international
affairs desk, which is what I call
my desk, we don't know. We'll conduct a thorough
investigation, through our southern bureau,
and let you know by suppertime tomorrow.

Keep the homefries burning. Keep the bellows
whistling on nostalgia's one live ember.
Nostalgia for itself. Do you remember
remembering? Kebab the fat marshmallows
of memory on the extended wire
coat hangers of desire
and hold them to the dry walls of drywall,
the bricked-in hollows.

The price of liberty is still eternal
vigilance. An obit in the *Journal*:
still ten a word. And the placeholder name
of our eternal vigil: duraflame.
The dead cannot procrastinate, and still
I'm having trouble making out my will.
Here's what I've got so far:

Four headstones leading

to my grave,

the last one reading

Burma-Shave.

The Name of the Game

So Bart and Lisa, thunderstruck with boredom,
decide to play a discontinued board game
called *Hippo in the House*. Of course the pivotal
hippo is missing but the bell still rings.

Between me and the boneless buffalo wings,
you say, releasing yet another single
into my subconscious, *that limp little
salad wasn't much of a bulwark.*

It's deep in the rotation now. In dreams
I work through variations on both themes,
slurring them to you from my lucid stupor:
That's one himp little house that needs some bonework,
I explain. But you're a heavy sleeper.

The New Ken

If Ken were here he'd tell us what to do.
Ken's a magician with this kind of shit.
We need him, and, somehow, he needs us too.

He'll come around. It's just that he withdrew
so suddenly it set us back a bit.
If Ken were here he'd tell us what to do.

The early Ken, I mean – the Ken who knew
that being here was to his benefit.
We need him, and, somehow, he needs us too,

but suddenly he'd rather see the shoe
fall from the other foot than see it fit.
If Ken were here to tell us what to do

we'd do it, and of course he knows it's true,
and knows he won't be here when we admit
we need him, but somehow he needs us to.

He sees it, but he needs to see it through
our eyes, or needs our eyes to see through it.
If Ken were here he'd tell us what to do.
We need him, and, somehow, he needs us too.

Notes Toward a Letter to Ed

You sent a doubled-sided leaf
of numbered matt prints from a sheaf
you found in a junk shop on Chartres
between Frenchmen and the French Quarter:
formals of local families, all
decked out for a Mardi Gras ball
in 1976, your guess is,
judging by all the flag-themed dresses.
Whoever coronates these krewes'
teenage royalty must use
the strangest and most strangely strict
criteria – the girls have picked
patterns and accents plainly based
on a shared sense of someone's taste:
floorlength and past-floorlength gowns
and headdresses suggesting crowns
without quite being them – a plume
apostrophizes one costume;
one supports a plastic staff
with an arpeggio of half-
and quarter-notes; and one has bunches
of wax grapes hanging from the branches
of its uncertain-looking lattice-
work headpiece. I didn't notice
the grapes at first because the daughter
has been retouched by runneling water
from a fire hose, the woman who sold you
the bundle for nearly nothing told you.
Somebody on the second floor
upset a voodoo candle or
an ancestor. It was the last
straw; her mother had just passed
and suddenly her life felt weighted
with decades of accumulated
junk, which obviously would've

been a challenge to get rid of
before the flood ... She seemed frightened
by her own words; it must have heartened
her to see you start to rummage
for the most fascinating damage,
which you found, and mailed to me
and other writer-friends to see
how we'd interpret it, and I'm
sorry I haven't had the time.

Fire Diary

Setup: what
do you get
when you cross
the road? Wait.
I placed my loss.

Setup: what's
so funny about
preserving the halitat's
natural habibut?

Nancy? Answer:
"Sir, you're drunkfish."
– Nancy Astor
Nancy, what's burning?
Nancy, you passed
out without turning
off the monkfish.
Nancy, the stove.
Nancy, you're an
alcoholic.

Nancy, this morning
the alc and hallcove
smelled like last
night's disaster
and minced garlic.
Nancy, that's
a nasty habibut.

Nasty, you can
have that bluefin
one of two ways:
Setup: why's
Nancy's place

like a halibut?
Answer: gutted.

Setup: what's
the difference?
I lost my place.
Answer: flooded.

***

Vulgar, like champagne
from a slipper,
there's been rain
on piles of paper.

The pimpled ceiling
looks like a river
that, while boiling,
has frozen over.

The books look fine,
but most were either
exposed at the spine
or flush with the wall,

and falling water
can only ride
a wall until
it meets a ledge,

so it will turn – whether
my books are dry –
on what I judge
my books by.

I look. Inside
each one, the dark,
stale, inscrutable
watermark.

Point Lobos

was something, but in pictures it's another
planet, with its three-inch facsimile
of cousin, second cousin and stepmother.
A handsome, figurine-scale family

clambers over the stone-studded faces
of newer stone, eccentric tidal scape,
sandmasonry, sand sanded into mesas,
committed by the kilning to its shape.

That day is in no danger. The sea otter,
belly-up in the bed of kelp, won't wake
to find a riptide taking him. The water
can't come for us. Those waves will never break.

Grandparents paid for everything. The sun
sent salutary beams from outer space,
and burned us, we would learn, but in this one
it only dulls the hard lines of my face.

No Daughter

No son. Son.
One life is mine;
my days can barely contain
themselves. I sleep in
the eggshell of zero.
My body says one.
The clock says one. I go
to the sink for water.
Son, no son.
Daughter, no
daughter.

A father has a son,
or daughter,
one born soon.
A son born early.

It's still early.
He has seen him through
the glass, seen
him clearly –
length of a pen,
radishy skin,
the clock says one,
the respirator.

In his sleep, when
he sleeps, he dreams
a daughter,
maybe a twin.
And he breathes at her.
One, two,
three, four, five,
she is alive, breathing in
the incubator.

No Daughter

Breath like water
drawn, drawn.
No son, son.
Daughter no daughter.

Thunder

It didn't matter because I had the muzzle
shouldered, indicating the whole sky,
when I let the insult of buckshot fly
into the larger argument of drizzle.

From where I stopped I could see the entire farm –
the sodden fields, the colder coming season,
my father in the milo stalks, my firearm,
the safety I had tested for no reason.

The Novel

We've all heard about Juanita – poor,
dear woman with her poor, dear woman act
metastasizing like a metaphor
into fact;

that benefactor of Topeka Teens
Making a Difference and the quiet third
shifts he was pulling, sealing smack glassines –
we've all heard,

even Nicole, whose novel never goes
anywhere because she isn't ready
to think the worst of characters she knows
haven't done anything to anybody.

Tiny Words in Photographs of
My Great-Great-Grandparents

I

Mary Hebbard Schenck: Nana's Nana.
Stranger in a familiar-looking chair.
Sixty years ago, the decorous manner
of ninety years ago, unsmiling for
the photograph, composed, hands folded on a
folded copy of the Sunday *Star*,
the letters *U.S.* in its tiny banner,
Bless This House behind her on the piano.

II

George Harvey, Mary Schenck's
husband. Brother Alva.
Sidewalk of pine planks.
Crates of PREMIUM JAVA,
Pearline Cleanser, produce –
ears of corn, heads of lettuce.
Horse apples in the street.

Moustaches like luna moths.
Not pictured: their mouths.
Nana said Auntie said
George would come home so sore
some nights he'd have to rest
before he could eat.
Dad has his workman's chest.

Oppressive worsted coats.
Collars at their throats.
The name of George's store
stenciled on the door,
I'd thought, but magnified
it's EAT QUAKER OATS.

Figurative North Topeka

for Ben Lerner

Seasonal graffiti crawls
up the overpass like ivy –
abstract names on concrete stanchions.
To the south, symbolic walls:
No Outlet signs along the levee,
idle river, idle tracks,
bypass, bluffside and the backs
of Potwin's late-Victorian mansions,
flush like book spines on that shelf.
Drunk on your late-Victorian porch
you promised me that if elected
you'd have the river redirected
down Fourth Street, to make Potwin search
North Topeka for itself.

I told you to retire *Ad Astra*
Per Aspera and put *For God's*
Sake Take Cover on the state
seal and flag – the license plate
at least, since we collect disaster
and loss like they were classic rods:
'51 Flood; '66 Tornado.
Even the foot-lit Statehouse mural
has a sword-bearing Coronado,
a Beecher's Bible-bearing Brown
and a tornado bearing down
on its defenseless mock-pastoral,
The Past. The present was still wet
when the embarrassed legislature
resolved that it would never let
John Steuart Curry paint the future.
He never did, although Topekans
would learn to let bygones be icons.

*   *   *

On Thursday, July 12, the rain
relented and the water rose,
darkened and stank more. The stain
is just shy of the second story
in what used to be Fernstrom Shoes.
That entire inventory
spent five nights underwater, gaping
like mussels on the riverbed.
Fernstrom spent the summer scraping
gobs of septic-smelling mud
out of eleven thousand toes.

On Friday the 13th, the Kaw
crested at thirty-seven feet.
They thought it might have cut a new
channel down Kansas Avenue.
One *Capital* reporter saw
a kid reach up from his canoe
and slap the stoplight at Gordon Street.

Porubsky's never did reclaim
its lunchtime clientele; the torrents
sent the Sardou Bridge to Lawrence
and there was no more Oakland traffic.
Business hasn't been the same
for fifty years now. Fifty-two.
Ad astra per aspera: through
the general to the specific.
You do what you want to do
but I'm not using North Topeka
in conversation anymore
because there is no north to speak of;
there's only mud and metaphor.

My Solipsism Is Superior to Yours

Because You Asked About the Line Between
Prose and Poetry

I've seen the local news: it's prose.
I prefer to look at the big picture
window – not because it shows
events exactly as they happen,
but because of the two recurring crows.

There's tragic laughter in the way they fly.
Some flaw in their understructure
compensates the most emphatic flapping
with very little loft. One barely goes
over and the other just gets by.

How to Write Autobiography

Avoid fried meats which angry up the blood
says Satchel Paige in his memoir, with all
the daffy precision of the *troubleball*
that left left-handers corkscrewed in the mud.
Presume Kingfish's innocence. Who's bringing
the allegation but *the alligator?*
And *who's that writing? John the Revelator.*
Don't interrupt the blind man when he's singing.
When writing, say or sing. Improvisation
was your whole life. *Authentic* is a game
that favors those who throw like trouble, name
like Adam and pronounce like Revelation.
Or fake it. Look at these italics, leaning
hard with the weight of someone else's meaning.

Vanguard

Here's what I remember: Coleman Hawkins
and I are sitting at a mahogany table
in the Village Vanguard, quietly talking.
He's finished a set in which he was unable
to summon even one unbroken tone
from the bell of his once-clarion saxophone.
But now that's over and he feels all right.
He's smoking because he's wanted to all night,
drinking cloudy cognac from a tumbler
and coughing ferociously; his voice is weaker
than his cough; he's barely audible, mumbling
to me because he knows I'm from Topeka.
He says, "That's where I learned to tongue my horn."
I know, and that's the only thing I hear.
It's 1969; in half a year
he'll be dead. In three years I'll be born.

"She's Gone"

David Ruffin's epitaph
reads, "Too Many Temptations."
It isn't worth a laugh,
but neither is ingratiation

worth the work. Some people stake
too many of their few
studio hours on stilted homage to
the ones who made them want to make.

Look, the fact of you
singing is a singular memorial.
There's no more irony in blue-eyed soul
than in a blue-eyed baby. Don't do

"Rolling Stone" tonight, okay, because
we all know who your papa was.

Misreading Pennsylvania

When the seventh salvo of silver flashes
cued the blue floaters for the seventh time,
blotting the smaller letters from their sashes,
I mispronounced "Miss Reading" – made it rhyme

with "misleading." Pissed off her press agent,
Miss Information, who steamed out to smoke.
But the style writers covering the pageant
called it an unconscious masterstroke.

So I became the Master of Near Misses.
The work kept coming. "You must be Miss Taken,"
I transproposed to the Pork Products Princess
panel, and you *should* have seen Miss Bacon.

They ate it up, though. It was liberating.
Within a month I didn't even need
my malaprompter. Cheating was creating.
Believing anything I couldn't read

I crushed my quadrifocals. People shed
their crosshairs and acquired a layer of fuzz.
Consequence came uncoupled. What I said
I saw, and what I saw was what I was.

"Please Please Me"

I don't love the Beatles. No one need
ever publish or anthologize
this poem now. To those who manage to read
this far into it, I apologize.

My girlfriend has said, not knowing she'd
end up in a fifth line, "Them's fightin' words."
I know. I know they gave me Alex Chilton,
who gave me the best of Big Star, through the Byrds.
I know their sound and am not ignorant of
their catalogue. I know it begins with "Love
Me Do" and takes a slow turn for the sallow,
maturing toward those white and mustard-yellow
albums everybody says are golden.

That's why I'm confident no one will see
this stanza. By now I've lost even readers
of poetry, who love their losing battles,
but not quite as much as they love the Beatles.

I believe in the many primacies of taste,
and in doing nothing to dislodge its nest
from a dependable cleft in the soul's one tree.
That's really why I don't love them: because
they make me feel like it's only me,
which is so unlike what so much music does.

"No Matter What"

I'm looking at *The Best of Badfinger*.
Their backdrop is an open book. A line
of thin, transverse horizon is the spine
or gutter, dividing pages of sky and water.

They were discovered by McCartney's father.
McCartney is the only publishing credit
below their signature single, "Come and Get It,"
which he in fact did everything but play.

George Harrison produced "Day After Day,"
their biggest hit, at Abbey Road for Apple.
The deaths began the year they left the label.

They might have been superimposed. The one
foregrounded at the far left, the dead ringer
for McCartney, has to be the singer.

Over his head, the golden imprimatur;
a sponsoring apple has replaced the sun.

What I Think

Most of it's over my own head.
It hangs around in the cartoon's
claustrophobic speech balloons
serving the sentences I've said.

I have trouble speaking plainly.
When I raise my hand and spread
my fingers, that's an asterisk.
When I said *bimbo*, I meant only
that you were a sort of gumbo/bisque.

No annotation. That's the trouble
with these graffiti laws. Precision
loves embellishment. The double-
negative, of course, affirms
itself in no uncertain terms.
Microsoft will never call
itself not hard or not unsmall
despite that antitrust decision.

The current and the tidal pressure,
perturbed by underwater structure,
give the river that troubled texture.

Hemingway, by the time he'd finished
writing, had written language off.
Only place-names were name enough
to mean themselves. Only Oak Park's
integrity was undiminished
by decades and quotation marks.

My Solipsism Is Superior to Yours

"Now, a high degree of satisfaction will typically result when the right balance between order and disorder is achieved ..." – Horace W. Brock

"... [M]usic is a character-forming force, and the decline of musical taste is a decline in morals. The *anomie* of Nirvana and REM is the *anomie* of its [sic] listeners." – Roger Scruton

The other night I played "Don't Lie to Me"
so loud I could hear Chris Bell say *fuck you*
to someone in the lull before the cue.
That's animus. I've got your anomie.
It's "In the Street." The prepositions pull it
three ways; three tinny vocals won't alloy;
and Bell at every break wants to destroy
his own arrangement, since he can't control it.
Steal your car, the disensemble sings.
Bring it down, pick me up, we'll drive around.
Is that an order, sir? What is the sound
of *it* when it refers to many things?
We've brought blunt instruments to beat the band
but can't disserve what we can't understand.

Bird Plays to a Cow

"A Swedish musician remembers a drive through farm country in a car full of musicians, one of whom told Bird that cows love music. Bird asked the driver to pull over ..." – Gary Giddins, *Celebrating Bird: The Triumph of Charlie Parker*

Fifty years from now
a writer, writing about me
playing to this cow,
will call the cow "he."
There's her udder, plain
as an udder, and yet ...
something about what people want
a cow, or an audience, to be.

Some painters haze the foreground
and render something in the middle-distance
unnaturally sharp, to remind the idiot looker
that this is a painting, not a pasture.

The writer will probably do
something self-referential, too,
and will almost certainly call the cow "bewildered."

"Bewildered." As though
I strode out here expecting her to nod
in time or stand on two hooves and applaud.
As though cows stand around waiting for something,
and not just anything, to come along.
Come on. What I do might confuse
you, but this cow was wildered when I got here.

To this cow there is only the plain fact –
    hot fence, sharp fence, shit,
    puddle, tuft of grass, golden horn

in the hands of the brown man
who wasn't here this morning and is here now –

and notes, too ...
after so much noise,
the plain fact of song.

My friend,
the bewildered one who's still in the car,
told me that cows dig music.
I choose to believe that. That's what I'm doing here.
She chews. That's what she's doing here.

"Larkin at Sixty"

I did the South Bank Show today. It went
no worse than I'd expected, though they spent
    rather too much time talking
about four-letter Larkin for my liking.

What will survive of me will no more live
than an appendix in preservative,
    and now it's clear to me
"They fuck you up" will be my Innisfree.

On the Smokestack

On the smokestack you can meet me halfway.
The smokestack is all smoke, you say.
Not exactly. Let's not forget
stack. Let's let the smokestack be, for a moment,
the ironic flagstaff of full employment.
Let's let it be some economic index's
index finger, indicating the sky.
There. Now it can be a cigarette.

We watch a woman board the train in shoes
so treacherous she has to keep an eye
on them when walking. Settled, she relaxes
and checks her messages. One is good news.
In your poem, what does the woman signify?

The world walks like a toddler, but it may
be getting there. It gets around okay.
What if the boneyard on the bluff
is really a skyline? The flecks
of moonstruck mica in the headstones
are office windows lit with banker's lamps.

You tell me that's the many sharpening
their bayonets for use upon the few,
but honestly I don't hear that happening.
I'll grant you the sound of whetstones
whining, but that could be for any purpose.
We need knives – even for some kinds of bread.

You tell me I hear cannons. I hear thunder.
You tell me we're on the outside looking under,
wishing we could switch seats with the dead
who ride around with us, just below the surface.
But I'm right here, looking at you.
The air is alive with cigarette smoke and dander.

McHenry Replies:

In January, Foday Sankoh's band
fled Freetown, amputating each third hand –
left, right, left – with machetes as they fled,
so when I think of the 6,000 dead
I try to think of someone who can carry
a shovel by the haft but cannot bury.
Connecticut will upset Duke tonight,
and Edgar Winter sells us Miller Lite.
Whether we act or not, we intervene.
When you say nothing I know what you mean.

Me and My Epoch

How can the story of life not be my story?
My mood obtains. The point of view is mine.
Life imitates, Art. Remember, when I'm dying
I'm dying to complete an allegory.
The census never slept. It strained the dead
from *decade* with its dispassionate seines –
autopsy, like auspice, written in the bones
in a longhand that was almost celebratory.
Me and meliorism say *Thank god that's over.*
Malaria, fire-bombing and the vast campaigns
of lava lie behind us, milestones.
Their road is a fallow frontage road, their bed
an oxbow obsolescence can't quite sever,
current that with its absence informs the river.

The Outstruments Are In

"Good Times"

words: Sam Cooke

Get in the groove and let the good times roll.
It might be one o'clock; it might be three.
I'm gonna stay here till I soothe my soul

if it takes all night long. You're beautiful,
beautiful as a song. You ought to see
yourself go, twisting to the rock and roll,

hands on your hips now, shaking like a bowl
of soup. I don't know much biology
but I'm gonna stay here till I soothe my soul.

Many's the day I've longed for you, to hold
you in my arms. How happy I would be.
Get in the groove and let the good times roll.

It doesn't have to be a miracle,
but there's one thing I want to guarantee:
I'm gonna stay here till I soothe my soul

if it takes all night long. I'll be made whole.
A change is gonna come. Bring it to me.
Bring it on home and let the good times roll.
I'm gonna stay here till I soothe my soul.

Hearing Myself Say the Name "C. Klafter"

But it will not be sought. It arrives
in my driveway as I'm departing for
the hospital. A tumbleweed, it thrives
only in neglect and sandy soil.

Germ of humor: in there like a star
is there in the night sky. It disappears
into its own history and haze
when you look at it, trying to meet its gaze.

When you wake, heaven-headed, and can speak
the syllables of its decrypted name
because you have described it with your sleep,
with the recovered lexicon of dream
and darkness, you can laugh. But you can't seek.

The Outstruments Are In

for Todd Hearon

The outstruments are in
you said, mock-drunk, and sure
enough they suddenly were –
Kevin with his guitar
and songbook, you with your
blond-bodied mandolin,
banjo and good ear,
Jack of Diamonds,
You Ain't Goin' Nowhere.

Redundantly, we kept
time with tambourines
and egg-shakers, or clapped.
And two friends of a friend
of Maggie's just sat there,
one in a folding chair,
one cross-legged on the floor,
insuppressible grins
fixed on their faces – pot
or something else, you thought.

People swayed, smoked, leapt
up for fresh drinks. Some
left for or returned from
another part of the party.
But these two remained
identically rapt
the whole evening, watching
you watch each other sing,
watching your left hand
walk down the skinny neck and
Kevin's dance on the body,

watching you each attend,
differently, to each string.

Finally one spoke –
across the room, over
the half-circle of singers
and their songbook refrain –
to the other, telling
what must have been a joke,
a dazzle of denotation
and virtuosic spelling.

For a while I watched you strain
to read their conversation –
obliviously bending
closer to it, attending
only to the fingers
and what they might be saying,
though you were still half sober
and hadn't stopped playing.

"Brick House"

For booty we come at the world ass-backward,
asking to be taken but not literally,
seeing ellipses, seeing nothing awkward
in casting them so quadrilaterally.
She is a brick house. I am not a car.
The difference is an idiom that relies
on other idioms that, likewise, are
idiom reliant. So it's no surprise
to hear some backseat frontman flub the line
we unequivocally call the refrain:
She's a freak, oww. And a freak, oww is *fine* –
a honey and a soothing sort of pain.
This one goes out to all you ladies, whether
you're stacked or built or simply put together.

Borrowing Milky-White for the St Paul's
Student Production of *Into the Woods*

The life-size papier-mâché
cow is laughable when it moves
because its legs don't. Stiffly, it rolls away
on the four swivel-wheels it has for hooves.

The wheels are unbuffed metal,
which makes the prop obstreperously rattle
across the washboard parking lot.
We wince. We're "rustling cattle."

But in the van, with its superior
vantage, there's no hurry.
Your school. Your afternoon. You ease us out,
gesturing at historic sites –
the Bulfinch building, the antiseptic dorms
where you endured third and fourth forms,
the dining hall, the stadium, the stagnant
pond that always stank, the cemetery
where your friends took dramatic black-and-whites,
the dean who'd been spectacularly pregnant
walking behind her son.

When you'd come through two years before,
you'd wanted to spend an hour like this, revisiting.
Jesse had seen a record store
and asked to be picked up when you were done.

You thank me for not being him, eliciting
a half-smile – a quarter-smile
really. It ends with my profile.
I can't countenance that guy just yet.
Your story relaxed its standards when he won
admission to the years before we met.
Now he'll always inhabit them. His face is

in their doorframes and shoeboxes. His drool
is in their pillowcases.

Memory is such a safety school.
Anyone can get in. Anything:
Jesse, some mossy headstones, a fake cow,
event and unevent, and now
the memory of you remembering
Andover, not wanting it again
exactly, but in the inexact way we want
most things –
inexactly the way we want them to have been.

The Rows

Immaculate Conception's central air
is broken. Nothing competes with our prayer.
Women bend their programs into U's
and fan themselves; the ones in skirts
slide them between their underthighs and the pews.

And Chris delivers himself like a fastball
down the aisle – wound up tight
because he's Chris, of course, but more so
today: like a hideless fastball, all
taut, thread-thin elastic, quivering ends.
As we rubberneck to smile
at him, though, he slows.
He eases himself, now, looking at the rows –

his groomsmen like a row of vases, white from black,
a row of easy faces, easy torsos,
easy the pinstripes in a row of vests.
He turns to face the rows of programs, waving; they look like oars.
His whole life, back and back.

Molly will take her familiar shape, he knows. But for now
she's a tiny burst of white in a distant door.
His concentration opens, and something we've never seen before
passes like a wave across his brow,

and he lets it, like a wave,
recede, and then he lets
his weight slide to his heels, and he rests.

West Concord

The phonebook says West Concord, but until
the fifties it was Millville, for the mill,
and from one of the bike paths you can still
make out the overgrown
remnants of a stone
foundation set into the streamside hill.

But if you're looking for them on a winter
afternoon, you'll probably encounter
a field trip from the Children's Learning Center,
and have to lag while they
caterpillar their way
through, because the paths become so slender.

West Concord: the phonebook is full of Millers;
the woods are full of giant caterpillars
on field trips; and the earth is full of cellars
waiting like understudies
to emerge, and everybody's
out there pushing something – stones or strollers.

Nursery Rhyme

We've seen our best intentions kill
the hardiest houseplants, including
a vine from Betsy's mother's wedding,
which had seemed indestructible until
it spent Christmas vacation on our sill.

I'm sure you see where this is going.
Now we've got this baby growing
in you, and we believe we've got
it covered – clothes, the roof, insurance – but
of course we have no idea what we're doing.

What can we do but have it, feed it,
keep it hatted and car-seated,
and try to temper its awareness
of temporariness, the big unfairness,
with love, as if these things were all it needed?

Let Me Get This Straight

The garden, grubbed and bumblebeed,
gardened;

the thistle pulled, the trumpet-vined
thistle pardoned;

the tumbleweed detained;
the humus harrowed;

the deadwood and the tumbleweed
wheelbarrowed

to the burn pile; to the compost pile,
the lemon peel
and melon rind;

the bare patch and the feeder seeded;
the bare patch watered;

the herb bed herbicided;

the hens fed and the hectored
bare hen slaughtered;

the hummingbird nectared.

Potscrubber Lullabies

I

The Potscrubber completes a cycle
so vigorous the knives were rattling,
and pauses, waking Evan Michael,
who finds all silences unsettling.

There's no resemblance. It's too early.
Everything is still so round.
But we've occurred to him as surely
as silence has occurred to sound,

and when he's finished sharpening
into himself, and when we've blurred,
we're going to go on happening
in silence like he's never heard.

II

I wore him like a broken arm
all summer, slung
from my right shoulder in a paisley hammock
so deep the sides closed over him.
When I walked he swung, and slept,
lulled by the time his body kept
against my stomach.
When I stopped I had to sing.

Sitting on Jane Kenyon's Headstone

There'd been a thaw and then another freeze.
I left the car by Route 4, thinking maybe
   the snowglaze wouldn't break,
but it was April and I had the baby,
   and we sank to my knees.

I know you didn't choose it for our sake,
but thank you for a headstone we can use
when I've misjudged the road and need to shake
   the ice-beads from my shoes.

The Wheelhouse

Here I am / standing at my kitchen window / and I am important
– parody of a typical submission, composed by an editor of *Poetry*
magazine

The house corrects its course each time I ease
the swan's-neck faucet four or five degrees
along its arc. And I could bring the whole
thing shuddering to a stop
in our side yard. We live at what is top-
ographically the bottom of the bowl

and get no cell-phone service. But the view
of rising gardens, with the overlay
of my reflection in the little bay
window by the double sink,
is fine, and even what I'd call commanding
in certain kinds of light, from where I'm standing.

Evan's been down for hours. His toddler-sleep
is instantaneous and channel-deep –
a kind of independence, although either
of us would quickly die without the other.

That's overwrought. I've had a drink
too many, probably. But I'm alone
with my excesses for the night. I've thrown
the deadbolts and there's nothing left to do
except the dishes. I turn on the cold
and hear the cargo shifting in the hold.

Notes

"Sockless Jerry Simpson," referred to in "The Incumbent," was a 19th-century Populist politician from Kansas. (See Thomas Frank, *What's the Matter With Kansas?*)

"Because You Asked About the Line Between Prose and Poetry" refers to and borrows from Howard Nemerov's poem of the same title.

"How to Write Autobiography" refers to "John the Revelator," a song by Blind Willie Johnson; to Leroy "Satchel" Paige, who was a great Negro League and Major League baseball pitcher; and to Kingfish, who was a character on the *Amos 'n' Andy* radio show, known for his malapropisms. (See Henry Louis Gates, Jr., *Colored People*.)

David Ruffin, referred to in '"She's Gone",' was lead singer of the Temptations at the height of their popularity. He died at age 50 under mysterious circumstances probably related to drug use.

The epigraphs to "My Solipsism Is Superior to Yours" come from articles that appeared in *The New Criterion*. The poem refers to songs by Big Star.

'"Larkin at Sixty"' refers to the poems "An Arundel Tomb" and "This Be the Verse" and paraphrases a letter Larkin wrote to Judy Egerton. (See Andrew Motion, *Philip Larkin: A Writer's Life*.)

The first six lines of *"McHenry Replies:"* refer to events that took place in Sierra Leone in 1999 and are generally, not specifically, accurate. Edgar Winter is an American rock musician who had a number of radio hits in the 1970s.

The songs quoted in '"Good Times"' are, in order, "Good Times," "Win Your Love for Me," "Twistin' the Night Away," "Shake," "Wonderful World," "That's Heaven to Me," "Another Saturday

Night," "Touch the Hem of His Garment," "A Change Is Gonna Come," and "Bring It on Home to Me."

The Potscrubber of "Potscrubber Lullabies" is a dishwasher made by General Electric.

Index of Titles and First Lines

A Note About the Author

Eric McHenry was born in Topeka, Kansas on April 12, 1972. He is a graduate of Topeka High School, Beloit College and Boston University, where he earned an MA in creative writing and won the Academy of American Poets Prize. His poems have appeared in *The New Republic*, *Harvard Review*, *Northwest Review*, *Orion*, and *Agni*. He also writes about poetry for the *The New York Times Book Review* and *Slate*. He is the associate editor of *Columns* magazine and a contributing editor for The Poetry Foundation. He lives with his wife and two children in Seattle, Washington.

Other Books from Waywiser

POETRY

Al Alvarez, *New & Selected Poems*
Peter Dale, *One Another*
B.H. Fairchild, *The Art of the Lathe*
Jeffrey Harrison, *The Names of Things: New & Selected Poems*
Joseph Harrison, *Someone Else's Name*
Anthony Hecht, *Collected Later Poems*
Anthony Hecht, *The Darkness and the Light*
Timothy Murphy, *Very Far North*
Ian Parks, *Shell Island*
Daniel Rifenburgh, *Advent*
Mark Strand, *Blizzard of One**
Deborah Warren, *The Size of Happiness*
Clive Watkins, *Jigsaw*
Richard Wilbur, *Mayflies**
Richard Wilbur, *Collected Poems 1943-2004*
Norman Williams, *One Unblinking Eye*

FICTION

Gregory Heath, *The Entire Animal*
Matthew Yorke, *Chancing It*

NON-FICTION

Neil Berry, *Articles of Faith: The Story of British Intellectual Journalism*
Mark Ford, *A Driftwood Altar: Essays and Reviews*
Richard Wollheim, *Germs: A Memoir of Childhood*

*Expanded UK edition